BESTSELLING CHRISTIAN BOOKS

- 51 Most Powerful Prayers by Ryan
  Christianity/Prayers, ISBN: 9789354990847
- A Christmas Carol by Charles Dickens
  Christianity, ISBN: 9788193545874
- A Cloud by Day, a Fire by Night by AW Tozer
  Christianity/Inspiration, ISBN: 9789354990854
- Absolute Surrender by Andrew Murray
  Christianity, ISBN: 9789389716269
- Awakened Imagination by Neville Goddard
  Christianity, ISBN: 9789389157086
- Be What You Wish by Neville Goddard
  Christianity, ISBN: 9789387669550
- Delighting in God by AW Tozer
  Christianity/Good & Evil, ISBN: 9788194748632
- Experiencing the Holy Spirit by Andrew Murray
  Christianity, ISBN: 9788194764809
- Feeling is the Secret by Neville Goddard
  Christianity, ISBN: 9789389157109
- How to be Filled with the Holy Spirit by AW Tozer
  Christianity, ISBN: 9789389157116
- In His Steps by Charles M. Sheldon
  Christianity, ISBN: 9789390492794
- Life of Christ by Fulton J. Sheen
  Christianity/New Testament, ISBN: 9789389716306

Search the book by its ISBN

BESTSELLING CHRISTIAN BOOKS

- Man: The Dwelling Place of God by AW Tozer
  Christianity, ISBN: 9789354990656
- Paths to Power by AW Tozer
  Christianity/Discipleship, ISBN: Forthcoming
- The Alchemy of Happiness by Al-Ghazzali
  Christianity, ISBN: 9789387669505
- The Imitation of Christ by Thomas À Kempis
  Christianity, ISBN: 9789388118057
- The Knowledge of the Holy by AW Tozer
  Christianity/Sermons, ISBN: 9789389157130
- The Law by Neville Goddard
  Christianity, ISBN: 9789390492886
- The Magic of Believing by Claudie Bristol
  Christianity, ISBN: 9789388118149
- The Magic of Faith by Joseph Murphy
  Christianity, ISBN: 9789388118743
- The Miracles of Your Mind by Joseph Murphy
  Christianity, ISBN: 9788180320743
- The Power of Awareness by Neville Goddard
  Christianity, ISBN: 9789387669406
- The Pursuit of God by AW Tozer
  Christianity, ISBN: 9789389157147
- Your Faith is Your Fortune by Neville Goddard
  Christianity, ISBN: 9789389157161

Search the book by its ISBN

GOD WORKS THROUGH FAITH

FAITH IN GOD CHANGES EVERYTHING

ROBERT A. RUSSELL

GENERAL PRESS

Published by

GENERAL PRESS

4805/24, Fourth Floor, Krishna House
Ansari Road, Daryaganj, New Delhi - 110002
Ph : 011-23282971, 45795759
E-mail : generalpressindia@gmail.com

www.generalpress.in

First Edition : 2023

ISBN : 9789354994388

Published by Azeem Ahmad Khan for General Press

Contents

Dedication

To the memory of my good friend and co-worker, W. V. Woollen, who turned possibilities into realities through his great understanding, vision and faith.

Introduction

This is the second in a series of books in which each title begins with the words, "God Works..." I do not apologize for the repetition in the title or in the content. The human mind tends to learn great truths, scientific principles, and mathematical facts slowly, or so my own experience leads me to believe. Can you remember your struggle with addition combinations? How many repetitions did it take for you to master the multiplication tables?

Parents are often impatient with the persistent questions of children about the facts of life which have been conscientiously presented to them, and sometimes attribute these to a morbid curiosity. It isn't that. It is merely an indication that the child has not been able to accept the explanation given him and to make it his own in one experience.

No day goes by that doesn't teach me more about the way in which God works and more about what the power of faith can accomplish.

I learn from my own experience, from observing the lives of others, and from reading the words of persons who have deep convictions. In this book, I have centered my discussion on faith.

–Robert A. Russell

CHAPTER 1

What Faith Is

Did you ever contemplate the things that happen through faith—not the things that could happen, or the things that might happen, but the things that do happen, the things that are happening now?

Where Did Faith Come From?

You were born with the characteristic of Faith, for it is inherent in man. Protected from the moment of your conception, you emerged into the world with the expectation of continued security. You accepted the loving care of your parents—food, shelter, guidance—without question.

You not only accepted but demanded in a loud imperious voice the things that gave you emotional and physical comfort.

You took your first steps in confidence in the loving hand that held you, and you were not too discouraged by a few bumps and tumbles. You smiled and expected a smile in return.

Today you walk to your work or drive or take a bus, expecting to arrive at your destination all in one piece. You accept a job, expressing faith in your potential. You marry with faith in the one you have chosen and faith in your power to provide for your family.

In other words, you have faith in yourself, and that is actually faith in the God within you. You eat food prepared by countless hands that you never see and wear clothing made by persons you will never know. You trust the taxi driver to take you to your destination, the barber to shave your face, and the cook to prepare your meals.

How do you know that the taxi driver won't take you to some out-of-the-way place and hold you up? Or that the barber will not cut your throat? Or that the cook will not poison your food? Because of your faith in your fellow-man and that too is faith in the one God, who according to St. Paul, *is above all, and through all, and in you all.*

Three Gifts Are Yours.—When man walked out from God's finished thought, he bore three gifts:

- **Life**—(energy, animation) by which to Live
- **Mind**—(the power to reason, select, understand, and know) by which to become aware of God, of himself and his environment

- **Faith**—(trust, confidence, assurance) by which to penetrate the invisible and to hold God's promises until they are realized in him and for him

What is Faith?

The St. James version of the Bible says *Faith is the substance of things hoped for, the evidence of things not seen.* Moffatt translates the words in this way: *Now faith means that we are confident of what we hope for, convinced of what we do not see.* What comforting words: *evidence, assurance, conviction, substance!*

Faith is the belief that you have the power to do all things. It is a magnetic power that attracts the answer to your prayer. Results do not come by chance, accident, or fate. They are molded by your faith in your power through God.

Faith is the glass under the faucet; it is the water wheel under the fall; it is the windmill adjusted to the wind; it is the sunflower facing the sun; it is the ear at the telephone. Success reduced to its lowest and simplest terms is faith expressed in action.

Faith is a mental attitude against which there is no possibility of contradiction. If that attitude is directed toward God, it becomes your ability to do anything. When you pray or treat, you have a right to expect an answer to that prayer or treatment, providing your conviction is in line with the nature of God.

Your mind, however, must be so convinced of its idea, it must so completely accept it, that contradiction or denial is impossible.

When you have absolute faith, there is nothing left in you to contradict your treatment.

Faith is the bridge between the physical and spiritual world. You have the privilege of crossing on it at will.

Faith not only makes old things new, but it is the point of contact between God and man. It is the means by which we identify ourselves with the Allness of God. Through our faith, God fulfills His promises. Through our faith, His Good becomes visible and usable. Desire is impressed upon the subconscious mind through feeling. Faith holds the idea of desire in Substance until it takes form.

Faith is the most dynamic and transforming force in man. To become mighty in the individual, it needs only a chance to exercise itself. As students of Truth, we must work for the highest and most complete state of faith, for faith is the wire along which Omnipotence moves. In that state, there is no longer anything in us to deny, doubt, or divide the Truth that we affirm.

We shall never perfect our faith, however, by talking about it, reading about it, waiting for it or wishing for it; we perfect it by applying it to every phase of our living, to the little as well as to the big problems in our lives.

Faith is not just a stirring—up of the imagination. It is an actual power which acts upon our words. It enables us to see things as God sees them, without blur or distortion.

Faith not only leads man into a definite course of action but opens the way for the Power to flow along the uncongested circuits of his thought. No longer hampered by doubts, fears, and worries, man becomes, as Emerson says, the "inlet and the outlet for all that there is in God." The highest faith is whole, continuous, triumphant, and victorious. It admits no contrary evidence, no fear, no opposition, no separation, and no limitation.

Hope says that it could happen or it might happen. Faith says that it will happen. It is the moving force in all creative processes. It is the agent of healing, of prayer, and of demonstration. It is the power to accomplish all things through Christ. All things are yours; and ye are Christ's; and Christ is God's. The man of faith experiences Wholeness. Thy faith hath made the whole, said Jesus to the woman who touched His garment in search of healing, to the blind beggar, Bartimaeus, and to the leper who returned to give glory to God.

Faith Is an Individual Power. Why did Jesus pin-point *thy* faith? Why not the faith of someone better trained or better equipped spiritually than you recognize yourself to be? He was showing us that the whole process takes place within the individual consciousness, within my consciousness if I am seeking the rewards of faith, within *yours* if you wish to experience Wholeness.

Why do we ask for another's help? Why do we have practitioners? When the evidence of the senses seems to overpower us, when we cannot see Reality through the cloud of false evidence, we are often impelled to seek the help of one whose vision is not obscured by our problem. But unless we meet the faith of the helper with one-hundred percent agreement, we are no better off than we were. *Our* faith is still essential.

The Answer Precedes the Problem.

Do you remember the place in which Jesus could *do no mighty works because of their unbelief?* Could healing not have taken place in Nazareth? The Truth is that the works were already done spiritually in that place as they are in all other places, but they had to await the recognition of the people concerned before they became visible on the material plane.

Do you see now why it is your faith that makes you *whole*? It makes you *whole* because in reality you are *whole* already. Your faith simply acts to reveal that which already is. The works come automatically to the heart that believes.

We do not see the Law of Faith, but we know its power by what it does. Our task is fourfold:

1. To become aware of that which eternally is—the Omnipresence of God
2. To claim the good we desire through faith, recognition, and realization
3. To accept the desire as fulfilled
4. To realize our Oneness with God until the feeling of fulfillment comes to us Faith is the realization that All Good Is In Instant Manifestation.

If our prayers were not answered, if our needs were not met before we prayed, there would be no point in praying. Jesus said, '*Before ye call I will answer and while ye are yet speaking I will hear*'. Whatever needs to be done is already done. Whatever is needed is already supplied. There is no Life apart from God, there is no Power apart from God, there is no Substance apart from God, there is no Health apart from God, there is no Being apart from God. There is only ONE Mind, Life,

Power, Substance, and Love in which we live and move and have our being. When we get the realization of this Truth, the whole outer world changes. Discordant factors are harmonized, problems are solved, difficult tasks are made easier, and diseases are healed. The tenor of our lives becomes harmonious.

Faith Acts on the Level of Our Consciousness—Life is a state of consciousness. Nothing can come to us except as consciousness. It is all that we are, all that we are aware of, all that we believe. We add to it or take from it with every experience. The level of our consciousness determines our faith and that level is of our own making. Faith is the starting point of every affirmation, prayer, and treatment; but without recognition of it as evidence of the Father Within without awareness of the closeness of our relationship to Him, without acceptance of His promises, without the realization of the Omnipresence of God, it is likely to end as wishful thinking, daydreaming, or mere desire.

As you rise in consciousness to the awareness of your Oneness with God, you will discover that there is no place for negation. It is not person, place, or thing. Therefore, it has no reason for being. Disease is a negative faith operating through man, but it isn't the man and therefore does not belong to him. That is why you must separate the belief from the believer in your own mind. If evil had as much power as good, the universe could not exist for a second.

According to Jesus, you must empty the mind therefore you can reach a heavenly state. *He that loseth his life shall find it.* When you lose your sense of personal power, the God Power awaits your use. If God is, He is all there is, and *all things* are possible to you because of your faith or conscious Oneness with Him. Now don't tell the world how wonderful it is until you have proved it for yourself. *Faith without works is dead.*

The primary purpose of spiritual therapy is not to make unhappy people happy, or sick people well, or poor people rich. It is not to solve problems or to establish better and healthier living conditions. These are results. The primary object is to help people realize the Presence of God.

Get Acquainted with God.—Eliphaz told Job in the midst of his suffering, *Acquaint now thyself with Him* [God] *and be at peace: thereby good shall come unto thee.*

To most Christians, God is a name rather than a warm and living Presence. We talk about Him, sing about Him, read about Him, preach about Him, and pray to Him; but very few of us take the time or trouble to get acquainted with Him. How, then, can we know Him *as a very present help in trouble*? When will we learn that faith cannot lift us any higher or take us any further than the level of consciousness on which we function? That it cannot take out of consciousness something which is not already there? Or that it cannot give us anything that is not already given?

If I want to know about electricity, how to use it and how to direct it, I associate myself with electricians who are experts with dynamos, motors, copper wires, switches and transformers; through them I come to the realization of electricity.

If I want to know about music, I associate myself with outstanding musicians, with musical instruments and compositions; through them I come to a realization of music.

If I want to know about painting and how to paint, I engage the best teacher I can find, I associate myself with artists, with paints, brushes, and canvas. I study the masterpieces of the world, and through all these, I come to a realization of painting.

If I want to get acquainted with you, I must identify myself with you. I must associate with you and be a companion to you. I must give you my thought and time. I must study your mind and your nature. If I am to understand you, I must know all about you. I must surrender to you.

How does one get acquainted with God? How does one get to know Him? Only by practicing His Presence. God must become to us a living, pulsating Presence. He must become as real as our friends or the members of our family are to us. We must know Him, not as a cold and lifeless name, not as a vague and misty personality, but as an actual, living Partner.

The first function of faith is to make God real—to make Him as real to us as He was to Jesus, John, and Paul. Where is God? Within each one of us. Not within us in the sense that He is within our body, our solar plexus, or our brain, but within our consciousness.

I and the Father are one.—When you realize that God is not in one place and you in another, when you understand your Oneness with Him and can say and believe *I and the Father are one*, your word will *accomplish that whereunto it is sent*, according to the promise. When you believe that your desire is already fulfilled, believe that what you are asking for is already yours, you have put your faith to work and what you seek will be manifested in your experience. You have the word of Jesus that this is so, for He said, '*What things so ever ye desire, when ye pray, believe that ye receive them, and ye shall have them… And all things whatsoever ye shall ask in prayer, believing, ye shall receive… Before they call, I will answer; and while they are yet speaking, I will hear*'.

There is nothing on earth you cannot have, nothing you cannot heal, nothing you cannot be if you have faith enough to accept the fact that what you are seeking is already yours. The fact that you can visualize a changed condition is proof of the Spiritual Reality of it. By your faith in the God with whom *all things are possible*, the desired condition materializes. *I can of mine own self do nothing... The Father that dwelleth in me, he doeth the works... He that believeth in me, the works that I do shall he do also... All things are delivered unto me of my Father.*

In this Oneness *all things are yours*. The ears of the deaf are unstopped, blind eyes are opened, diseases are healed—not by using the spiritual to heal the physical, not by using will power to force others to conform to your way of thinking, not by the application of brute force, but by the uncovering of the Perfection that is already there.

Too long have we had God in one place and man in another. Too long have we kept apart that which God hath joined together.

Do you understand? You who are reading these lines? You do not have to acquire any-thing, buy anything, or create anything. You have only to accept your Oneness with Him through faith.

Believest thou not that I am in the Father and the Father in me?... I and my Father are one... The Father that dwelleth in me, he doeth the works. Could there be a stronger statement of Oneness, of Integration? God is all Life; He is your Life. God is Mind; He is your Mind. God is Power; He is your Power.

Why is the consciousness of Oneness so necessary to the perfect outworking of faith? Because it supplies the inner forces of faith. It acts as a magnet to draw to itself everything it needs for expression. Solomon said, '*With all thy getting, get understanding*'. Without this inner force, the consciousness of the Allness-of-God and our Oneness with Him, faith is partial, limited, and incomplete. It becomes what some teachers refer to as "blind faith" in contrast to understanding faith.

Did you ever try to demonstrate over a problem while keeping your attention on the problem? What happened? You still had the problem but in a magnified form.

How Big Is Big? Jesus' one and only formula for meeting trouble was *Have faith in God.* With faith you can solve the apparently irreducible problems and remove the presumably insurmountable obstacles in your life. You can dominate every circumstance, you can open every door. It doesn't matter what the circum-stance, condition, or problem may be, *If ye have faith as a grain of mustard seed, ye shall say unto this mountain, 'Remove hence to yonder place'; and it shall remove; and nothing shall be impossible to you.*

Jesus likens human problems and troubles to moun-tains, but He says that if you have faith, you can remove these mountains. You can cause them to be swallowed up and lost sight of for-ever. All your sickness and troubles can be re-versed when you have a radical belief in God and an unqualified and unquestioning acceptance of the fulfillment of your desires. But you must trust your faith in the same way that the air-borne infantryman trusts the parachute that is bringing him to earth.

If ye have faith as a grain of mustard seed... nothing shall be impossible to you. Jesus did not say that fulfillment depends upon argument, reason, theology, logic, or a particular concept of God, but upon faith. Faith the size of a mustard seed is not a lot of faith, but note the power Jesus assigned to it. Of course, the mustard seed has an amazing potential for growth. So does the small faith that you plant in the subjective mind if you tend it carefully. Perhaps the faith you have now is just enough faith to let you try faith. Tend the seed with love and confidence. Water it with persistency and tenacity. Shelter the tiny growth from the cold winds of negative thought.

Visualize the effect in your life of faith in action. See yourself using it, living in it, expressing it. Accept the promises made to those who believe as made to you personally. Know that any desire you hold in faith is a Reality in Spirit, existing from the moment you conceived it and eagerly awaiting its manifestation in your life. Put your faith to the test. Exercise it. Let it grow.

Why did Jesus use the mustard seed as a symbol of faith? To show the infinite power of even a little faith. The mustard seed is not only one of the smallest of seeds, but it is one of the most powerful and productive of creative things. And so it is with the little bit of faith.

With Jesus, the lesser faith was always the promise of the greater faith. It doesn't matter how small your faith is, if you believe in it, if you have faith in it, if you keep it alive, if you keep it in motion, it has to grow.

Never allow yourself to minimize your "mustard seed" of faith. Never allow yourself to think of it as inadequate. Know that you have it and that you couldn't lose it if you wanted to. Praise it. Let it grow. It will do wonders for you; *nothing shall be impossible to you.*

Let us think of it in this way. In the "mustard seed" stage, my faith is like a little candle in the mind. It gives forth a certain amount of light. But it is governed by impersonal law; it works the way I use it. If it works slowly for me at first, that is because my expectations and mental equivalents are small. I need to step them up. I know that a little steam will lift the lid of a tea kettle but a lot of steam will lift tons. The Law of Faith is just that simple:

With what measure ye mete, it shall be measured to you again. The manifestation of my faith is not measured by the size of my faith but by the acceptance, belief, or mental equivalent which I hold. If I want a 500 candle power light, I must have a 500 watt bulb. If I want the *good measure, pressed down, and shaken together and running over,* I must present a large measure.

Thousands of people go every year to Shrines and Blessed Pools believing that they have some magic power to heal. Hundreds who have faith are healed through contact with these places. But thousands return unhealed because they do not have the necessary faith.

The Law of Faith

According to your faith—your faith in God, your faith in yourself, your faith in your goal, your faith in your ability, you get results. The man of little faith gets small results; the man of big faith gets large results.

According to your faith, be it unto you. That is just like saying that a gallon jug will hold only a gallon of water. We can never go beyond the realization of our mental equivalents. We shall never experience a good which is beyond our capacity to conceive and to receive. This whole problem of belief and realization is just like using the muscles. Today we can lift twenty pounds; tomorrow we can lift twenty-five. But there is no limitation to our capacity for spiritual growth. We always express what we are. As much goodness as we can accept, that much we can demonstrate. Sickness doesn't have to be, but until we know it doesn't have to be, it will be. When we know that limitation doesn't have to be, there will be nothing to be limited.

All that I have is thine.—Are you a beggar sitting on a bag of gold? Are you slumbering on the brink of the Infinite power? Behold! You stand this day at the entrance to a land of tremendous possibilities. *Son, thou art ever with me, and all that I have is thine.* This *all* is yours if you have the faith to accept it, if you believe that you already have it, if you let it manifest AS YOU, *Seek ye the Lord while He may be found. Call ye upon Him while He is near. When is He near?* When you accept your Oneness with Him, when you know that you have no Mind, Life, Substance, or Power apart from Him.

What a light would come into our lives, what invincible power would come into our minds, what a cleansing of the soul and body would result if we made use of this inner force of faith. *New wine*, Jesus called it—wine that bursts old wine skins of limited patterns and demands a new consciousness to hold it. We don't need new faith or more faith to be transformed. We need only to renew our faith in the faith we al-ready have.

Come, my friend. Make your contact with God through faith. The way of attainment is wonderfully simple and accurate. It is not the way of the conscious mind, of human thinking, or the way of teachers. It is the way of Spirit. *I am that I am. I am the way. In all thy ways acknowledge him.* In all thy ways acknowledge His Presence, and It will guide you into all truth.

In him we live and move and have our being. Can God be any closer to us than our consciousness of Omnipresent Good? Can He be any closer than *here*? Then rest from your anxious labors; release your tensions and your fears. In the consciousness of Oneness is your salvation.

When you pass from belief to realization, when you *live and move and have your being* in Omnipresent Good, Omnipresent Good lives and moves and has its being in you.

How much longer are you going to wait before you release this tremendous power within yourself? *Have faith in God.*

Ways to Strengthen Faith

1. Be expectant, confident, and optimistic.
2. Keep your enthusiasm strong; never allow yourself to be discouraged or depressed.
3. Charge your mind with interest, enthusiasm, ambition.
4. Keep your ambition and aspiration high; cultivate patience and perseverance.
5. Keep your imagination centered in what you want and keep your faith moving toward it.
6. Keep your consciousness expanding, growing and moving to higher levels.
7. Be positive in your thought, feeling, and action.
8. Accentuate the positive in every situation. Never allow yourself to dwell upon misery, sickness, operations, symptoms, reverses, misfortunes or bad luck.
9. Never depreciate, criticize, minimize or speak disparagingly of yourself. Never dwell upon your mistakes. Think always of yourself as growing, expanding and becoming more efficient, resourceful and dynamic.
10. Look for the good in everything and everybody. Refuse to recognize anything but the good.
11. Seek the best of everything and know that your mind will produce it.
12. Think in large terms. The more you expect, the more your faith will bring to you.
13. Convince your mind that what you seek is already here, that it is yours now.

14. Train your mind to think in terms of abundance; never allow it to dwell upon lack or limitation in any form.
15. Stimulate your faculties and talents by increasing your demands upon them.
16. When you meet trouble of any kind, refuse to be worried or disturbed by it. Know that you are bigger than any adverse thing that happens to you and have the power to overcome it.
17. Meet every problem with the conviction that it is already solved. See it as an opportunity to prove God.
18. Face every difficulty with courage, strength, and fortitude; determine to turn it to good account.
19. Know that you have the power to adjust anything, change anything, correct anything, overcome anything, or subdue anything.
20. Act always with the Truth; and never allow yourself to compromise with evil. If the Truth is to make you free, you must rely upon it. You must pass from belief to trust.
21. Believe the unbelievable. God goes all out for you when you go all out for God.

CHAPTER 2

How Faith Works

Through faith we understand that the worlds were framed by the word of God, so that things which are seen were not made of things which do appear.

The American Translation of the Bible clarifies these words: *It is faith that enables us to see that the universe was created at the command of God, so that the world we see did not simply arise out of matter.*

Moffatt translates the same passage in this way: *It is by faith that we understand that the world was fashioned by the word of God, and the visible was made out of the invisible.*

Before life becomes meaningful, before religion has any significance, you must face these questions:

1. Do you recognize man as more than physical, more than intellectual?
2. Are you also aware of the spiritual man?

3. Do you recognize that there are spiritual forces at work in the world?

Your answer, of course, is yes or you would not be reading this book. You would not be searching for a satisfactory explanation of God and of your relationship to Him. You would not be trying to find a pragmatic religion. You would have no desire to learn more about Spiritual Laws, no ambition to grasp the means of communication with Spirit which are available to you. You would not want to know how faith works.

The persistence of man's recognition of his need for God and his unceasing search throughout the ages are proof in themselves of the Reality of the God he seeks. What he calls God is not particularly important. What he does with his belief is of supreme importance, for it determines the circumstances of his life, the conditions under which he lives.

Faith Works Through Acceptance.—A Unitarian minister, James Freeman Clark, once said, "All the strength and force of man comes from his faith in things unseen. He who believes is strong; he who doubts is weak. Strong convictions precede great actions. The man strongly possessed of an idea is the master of all who are uncertain or wavering. Clean, deep living convictions rule the world."

Someone has defined faith as "the unconditional acceptance of the truth of our affirmations and an absolute belief that our desires will be fulfilled." Faith is not presumption but assumption. It is believing something which the conscious mind says is not true.

Volumes could be written on the subject, but let us try to boil the process down into a few words: To be successful in faith we must not only assume (believe) that God is able, willing, and eager to help us, but we must also accept our responsibility to cooperate with Him. How do we cooperate? By our realization and trust that He is fulfilling our every expectation NOW.

Our work is to make those facts real to our minds. I can speak the word of Peace, Health, or Prosperity, but unless my feeling supports the word that I speak, it accomplishes nothing. It is only when my word and my feeling unite that I become One with the Power. Why is this true? Because feeling is the shock that sets the Divine Energy in motion.

There is a powerful Spiritual Law at work here. It doesn't make any difference what your problem or difficulty may be, if you will bring your faith and your feeling to bear upon it, if you will realize that right now and always, there is an Infinite Power waiting to fulfill your slightest or greatest wish, you don't need to seek the solution. It will seek you.

The Law of Faith.—*According to your faith be it done unto you.* The Universal Response will always be in direct ratio to the degree of your expectation. *To him that hath* [the consciousness of fulfillment] *shall be given. From him that hath not* [this consciousness] *shall be taken away even that which he hath.* If you expect much, you will receive much. If you expect little, you will receive little.

The Law Must Be Fulfilled.—The Law works equally well, however, when It is brought to bear on negative thought and feeling. If you concentrate on ill-health, poverty, loneliness, injustice, and futility, these conditions manifest in your life *according to your faith.*

The first thing to determine is the kind of faith you have. When you wish good to materialize, you must have a positive, constructive faith. Then you are in a position to strengthen and develop it.

Perhaps your faith is only the residue from the background of your childhood; maybe it is a little shriveled from lack of use or tattered and worn from misuse. You still have it, however. All it needs is your awareness of its power, your recognition that you already have it in your possession and the opportunity to express itself in action.

Assume now that you have all the faith in God that you need. Then act in accordance with this assumption. Every affirmation, thought, feeling, word and action that expresses faith impresses faith upon the inner mind. As the subconscious accepts the impression, it will set in motion forces that are faith-producing.

When we fill the subconscious mind with faith—thoughts of faith, feelings of faith, memories of acts of faith—by some mechanism of creation, we have faith. The Law of Action and Reaction is at work. The impression is an act of faith; the reaction expresses the power of faith.

The subconscious mind is the creative phase of mind. It acts on what is given to it but does not originate anything. But not every thought and feeling penetrates to the subconscious fortunately.

We cannot always determine which of the many impressions we receive in the course of the day will go beyond the conscious mind—the mind of the senses—the top of the mind. Whatever passes through this mind and finds lodging in the subjective mind is quite likely to be pregnant with feeling of some kind. But we have learned that we can deliberately plant in the subconscious mind the mental equivalent of the thing we should like to have objectified in our lives, that we can nullify thought that has been implanted for years, and that we can protect ourselves from the effect of a disastrous thought if we are aware of our danger at the time it threatens.

God Works Through Silence.[1]—That is why it is a good idea to spend a certain amount of time each day impressing faith upon the subconscious. We call this period the Silence. When you are alone and relaxed, shut out the world, become very still and make your declaration of faith. Even though you have a hard time affirming faith, affirm it anyway. Even if you don't feel that you have it, say that you have it. Say, "I have faith in God."

Say it positively and with feeling. Feel it down deep in your heart. Know that every thought you think and every word you speak contains the mountain-moving power of faith. Concentrate on the meaning of the word. Visualize its effect in action in your life. See yourself moving in a world in which you meet men of faith, men in whom you put your trust—a world in which you prove your own faith by the authority with which you speak and act, by your calmness and poise and fortitude under difficulties, by your resiliency when stress has been removed—a world in which *All things work together for good.* The promise reads, *All things work together for good to them*

1. See God Works Through Silence

that love God. Paul told the Galatians that nothing availeth anything... but faith which worketh by love.

Thanks be to God.—We speak of enlarging our faith, but the only way in which we can do this is by enlarging our mental equivalents, by increasing our demands and by adding the quality of gratitude. When we believe that God wants through us the thing we want, we are ready to give thanks in advance.

George W. Wilson says, "Possession follows the feeling that you do possess the things desired, and that feeling is made stronger if you will express gratitude for the possession." *What things so ever ye desire... believe that ye receive them, and ye shall have them.* When one is grateful for something he has not yet seen or touched or experienced as the result of his conviction that it already exists, his gratitude will hasten its arrival.

Have you ever noticed that praise of a dog brings out the best in him and that praise of a man inspires him to be and to do his best? So it is with faith. Many delayed healings have come when the sick have applied the power of praise and thanksgiving.

The Conscious Mind Is an Agent.—There is a tendency on the part of some meta- physicians and schools of thought today to disregard the conscious mind—to negate it or to ignore its activities. This is, of course, foolish on the face of it. The conscious mind is not only the mind of awareness and recognition, but the instrument that starts the mind working in the chosen field of thought. It senses and selects those ideas which it wishes to entertain. Jesus said, *Ye shall know the truth, and the truth shall make you free.*

Without the activity of the conscious mind, we cannot know or be aware of anything. Acceptance of Truth begins in the conscious mind as recognition or awareness; it is conveyed to the subconscious mind through realization or feeling. We become aware of ideas. Through conscious thought we impress these ideas upon the subconscious mind. This does not mean that we are going to use the conscious mind to solve problems, heal disease, or to demonstrate prosperity. We are going to use it for the purpose for which it was intended—an agent to help us become aware of the Omnipresent Good.

Science tells us that within the human body there are more than fifty million cells, each of which is a miniature universe and each of which lives its own life. The Psalmist declares that *Heaven and earth are full of thee,* which means that GOD IS EVERYWHERE EQUALLY PRESENT. God actually lives in each one of these cells at the same time. Each one is a manifestation of God Consciousness. If we live in the Consciousness, *I and my Father are one*, our bodies are vibrant with Life, Spirit and Health. In the presence of Perfection, every cell expresses that Perfection.

We do not treat *against* arthritis, neuritis, appendicitis, tonsillitis, sinusitis, bursitis, colitis, nephritis, or any other specific physical difficulty. In fact, the more we treat against a thing, the more we fasten it upon ourselves and the more real it becomes to us. Why is this true? Because a treatment against anything is virtually a treatment *for* that thing. Disease is the effect of a cause implanted in the subconscious mind. We overcome disease by realizing that the body is Spiritual Substance—an extension of Spirit in perfect form.

I and the Father are one.—The great purpose of Jesus' message was to teach us to realize our Oneness with God. When Peter recognized and acknowledged the Christ in Jesus, the Master blessed him. *Lazarus is dead,* said Jesus, but nevertheless He commanded, *Lazarus, come forth.* And so He commands today.

Throw off the grave clothes of your former self. Lift yourself a bit closer to the Allness-of-God. Why repeat the race history of Adam? Why carry yesterday's ills, problems, and disappointments over into today? *Know ye not that the prayer of faith shall save the sick?* Hath it not been revealed to you that *the Son of man is come to save that which was lost?*

Be still and know.—The most wonderful Statement of Being known to man is *I and my Father are one.* Meditate upon it and make it your own. Take it into the stillness of your consciousness and let God reveal Himself to you. *Be still and know that I am God.* Let His Life, Substance, and Power flow through you AS YOU. Open your mind to the truth of your Oneness with Him. Apply it to your body. *Yet in my flesh shall I see God.* Make your contact with Him and say:

> I KNOW THAT MY BODY IS SPIRITUAL SUBSTANCE. NOTHING CAN FASTEN TO IT THAT COULD NOT FASTEN TO PURE SPIRIT. SPIRIT COULD NOT BE SUBJECTED TO DESTRUCTIVE ACTION; THEREFORE, NOTHING DESTRUCTIVE CAN OPERATE IN ME. THE INFINITE PERFECTION OF SPIRIT IS NOW WORKING IN EVERY CELL OF MY BODY,

FOR I AM ONE WITH IT. I ACCEPT MY HEALTH, MY WHOLENESS, WITH GRATITUDE.

Actually there are no healers of disease; there are only revealers of health. Get rid of the festering, smoldering, soiled, smelly, disease producing thoughts in the mind. Empty out all the mental waste that has been accumulating for years. Flush out all the enmities, doubts, fears, jealousies, and worries by reversing them.

Claim your Oneness with God, and all these poison pockets will be drained. You will understand for the first time the meaning of Jesus' words: *Yet in my flesh shall I see God.* When Naaman the Syrian dipped in the Jordan seven times, his flesh became as pure as that of a little child. So will ours when we know each new cell as perfect.

Dr. Alexis Carrel of the Rockefeller Institute says in *Man the Unknown*, "There is unquestionable proof of the efficiency of prayer in the cure of all diseases." The documented story of the cure of tuberculosis, cancer, and other stubborn diseases by its use has been told many times.

Praying without ceasing is the constant recognition of our Oneness with God. Healing emanates from a consciousness of Wholeness. Health is a state of consciousness, a creative, up building force that can turn weakness into strength, disease into ease, limitation into plenty. It is this realization that makes prayer effective and practical. When you get yourself out of the way of the divine circuits, the King of Glory will come in. When you find God within yourself, the prayer will be answered.

"Prayer," says Kahlil Gibran in *The Prophet*, "is but the expansion of yourself into the living ether. When you pray, you rise to meet in the air those who are praying at that very hour, and whom save in prayer you may not meet. Therefore let your visit to the temple invisible be for naught save ecstasy and sweet communion. I cannot teach you to pray in words. God listens not to your words save when He himself utters them through your lips."

Prayer is the realization of our Oneness with God and the acceptance of the tremendous power this realization gives us.

Someone has likened faith to a bicycle. "It stands upright only when it is in motion. The minute it stops moving, it flops on its side." Faith must be kept in motion if it is to have power. It must be exercised to be of use.

Open mine eyes.—Have you found God? Where are you seeking Him? *God is a spirit,* said Jesus. But no one has ever seen Spirit. If you say, "I will believe only what I see," you are living in darkness. You are in bondage to yourself, and you cannot know anything beyond yourself. You cannot know God. You cannot know Christ. You cannot know life. You cannot know Power. No one has ever seen God, Life, or Power.

If you believe only what you see, you must doubt your own existence. You have seen the house in which you live, but you have never seen yourself. What you see in the looking glass is but the form of your outer self. All you see of your loved ones is the body house in which they live. The Real Self you have never seen.

If we accept the appearance for the fact, we are denying our true selves. We exclaim with Job, *Behold I go forward, but he is not there; and backward, but I cannot perceive him: On the left hand, where he doth work, but I cannot behold him: He hideth himself on the right hand where I cannot see him.*

Man is... full of trouble.—Are you easily discouraged? Do difficulties pile up on you to such an extent that you tend to lose heart? Then remind yourself of Jesus' words, *In the world ye shall have tribulation* [trouble]: *but be of good cheer; I have overcome the world.*

Settle this thing in your mind once and for all. Did God promise a soft and easy life? Did He promise that life here would be a bed of roses? Did He say that there would be no crosses to bear, no problems to solve, no obstacles to climb over, and no vicissitudes to meet? He did not.

Then what is His plan for us? We have it in Jesus' own words, *Be not conformed to this world: but be ye transformed by the renewing of your mind.* In other words, Be in the world but not of it. Go out and live life. Fight the good fight of faith. Keep the faith. *Take unto you the whole armor of God* [Consciousness of Truth] *that ye may be able to withstand in the evil day, and having done all, to stand.* Of course you will have trouble in an unfinished world, but be of good cheer; I have overcome the world. [I have given you the Mind and Power with which to meet the world.]

It is true that you can skip a lot of trouble on the experience plane. In fact, you can often transform trouble by letting *this mind be in you which was also in Christ Jesus.* You can ward off a lot of grief by practicing the Presence of God. But trouble touches everyone at some time. In the world ye shall have tribulation because it is that kind of world.

Then why be negative, pessimistic, and tragic about it? Why single yourself out as a special target for trouble, saying as it hits you, "Everything happens to me"?

After all, we are not like the bewildered little boy who was lost in a Dry Goods Store. When a sympathetic floor walker stopped to ask what was wrong, he replied, "Please, Sir, have you seen a lady without a little boy who looks like me?"

We, sorely tried and troubled as we are at times, do have a Father and "closer is He then Breathing and nearer than hands and feet." *In Him we live, move, and have our being... Being justified by faith, we have peace with God through our Lord Jesus Christ... And not only so, but we glory in tribulations also.* Perfect as this statement is, St. Paul went a step further. He went on to say: *And we know that all things work together for good to them that love God.*

Do you see what the Apostle is trying to get over to us? It is simply this: No matter what befalls us, the secret of meeting it lies in bringing the power of God to bear upon it. If we face trouble with the desire to learn from the experience, we shall rise victorious. If it were not for trouble, there would be little mental or spiritual growth.

Channing Pollock, the great playwright, once said, "Men and motor cars go forward by a series of explosions. A beautiful motor car cannot fulfill its function until it has a series of internal explosions. Just so a human being with conflicts and difficulties to overcome gets somewhere and becomes someone."

Make Your Agreement.—The first step in dealing with trouble is to agree with it. *Agree with thine adversary quickly whiles thou art in the way with him*, says Jesus. In other words, accept trouble as one of life's inevitables in the world mind, see it as carborundum under the knife, and realize that it can minister to the soul's higher good.

Crises, failures, hardships, pain, suffering, opposition, and injustice are nothing more than explosions in the mixing chamber of the mind. Agreement not only robs them of their power but takes the fear, fire, and sting out of them and conditions the mind and life so that God can do greater things for us.

St. Paul said, Put on the whole armor of God. If the explosions tear you apart, you have not made your agreement with trouble. You will not be *able to withstand in the evil day.* St. Paul did not say, "*Put on part of the armor of God*" but specified the whole armor of God. You must give Him your whole heart, mind, soul, and strength. "The faith that saves," says John A. Redhead, "is the total response of the whole self to the will of God. It is the response hold the mind in belief, the heart in trust, the will in conduct."

I have known all kinds of people in all kinds of trouble, but it is only those who wear *the whole armor of God* who triumph over it. Do you see why agreement is so important in meeting trouble? It is one of the great factors in every successful demonstration. It determines whether trouble makes or breaks us, whether we go up or down.

The next step in meeting trouble is to cleanse the mind. Drop the trouble for the time being an you would drop a hot potato until it cools. Get clear away from it in your thought. This may take time, but keep at it. To receive the answer to any problem you must not only seek guidance, but must also present an open and untroubled mind ready to receive it. The solution cannot come while the mind is running like a trip hammer.

Be still and know that I am God. In quietness and in confidence shall be your strength. Get the consciousness of His Presence. See Him walking by your side. Know that you are surrounded by a Creative Mind that receives the impress of your thought and acts upon it. Know that you are in this Mind and that this Mind is in you.

Don't discuss your trouble with others and don't ask for advice; seek the answer within. If the subconscious state of your thought denies what your conscious thought says, it neutralizes the conscious thought. That is why St. Paul told us to *pray without ceasing.* To get results you must pray until your conscious thought believes and the subconscious thought no longer denies. You must pray until all doubts are removed. Treatment is a mental and spiritual adjustment; it is conditioning the mind so that it no longer refutes the idea of Perfection embodied in the treatment.

It is important to seek God's guidance in every problem, but we must first make sure that we are actually and wholeheartedly putting our problem in God's hands. Let us be childlike enough to believe that He will give us a definite and clear cut answer. It doesn't make any difference how difficult or how pressing the problem may be, it will ultimately disappear or be solved.

If you can be calm and collected in the midst of trouble, you will triumph over it. If you can fill your mind with the precious qualities of courage, confidence, and faith, nothing can defeat you. When the subconscious mind gets a new idea (when the idea takes possession of the conscious mind), it gets you. When you empty the subconscious of all adverse, tense, troublesome, and distorted thoughts and fill it with thoughts of life, power, victory, and optimism, the whole tenor of your life will change.

"But this is such tedious work!' you say. That in right, but so is anything that is worthwhile and lasting.

Don't be misled by the printed or spoken word. Many people say to me after listening to a lecture, "It sounds so easy when you tell us about it," and I know that is true. Faith is easy to understand but hard to apply. If it were otherwise, Christianity would soon lose its power. Faith is a challenge. If you are *going* to say the prayer of faith, you must not only back it up with acceptance, belief and trust, but, you must empty your mind of everything that contradicts or denies the prayer. That is why St. Paul said, *our conversation is in heaven.*

It is difficult to think and speak constructive, positive, happy, victorious, life giving words when the mind is filled with anxieties, apprehensions, antagonisms, antipathies, doubts, criticisms, and fears. Just when some great challenge or opportunity comes along which would enrich our lives or improve our circumstances, we are stopped dead in our tracks by a sense of doubt, fear, or inferiority. Some sinister thought wriggles up out of the subconscious mind and says, "Beware! This is not for you. You are not equal to it. You do not have what it takes. Let it alone."

Let not your heart be troubled.—Are you in some kind of difficulty right now?

Then start drawing upon your faith. Face the difficulty and say:

> GOD IN THE MIDST OF ME IS ABLE TO CONQUER THIS THING. HE IS DOING IT NOW. I HAVE FAITH TO MOVE MOUNTAINS, AND I AM CALLING UPON THAT FAITH NOW. I HAVE THE COURAGE TO CONQUER AND SUBDUE ANY ADVERSE THING.

But here comes that voice again, "You are only kidding yourself. You are scared stiff. You haven't any courage and you know it."

How are you going to silence this voice? You are going to challenge it every time it speaks. You are going to make it tell the truth. Say positively, forcefully, and with feeling:

> SUBCONSCIOUS MIND OF ME, I AM TIRED OF YOUR LIES, AND I COMMAND YOU TO TELL THE TRUTH. I COMMAND YOU TO RESTORE MY COURAGE AND FAITH, AND I COMMAND YOU TO DO IT NOW.

Speak as one having authority. Let the subconscious know that you mean what you say.

Imagination Is a Gift.—Call upon your imagination. See yourself as you wish to be. See yourself possessing the things you desire to possess. Marcus Aurelius once said, "A man's life is dyed by the color of his imagination." Imagination is the process of projecting images upon the screen of the mind. You don't have to go through a lot of mental gyrations and exercises.

You don't have to argue, reason, or divide. You just make a picture—you become aware of something—you know something.

Raise the Level of Your Consciousness.—Would you have God? Then you must accept Him. You must become aware of Him. You must be conscious of Him. Do you see that? Do you understand it? Let me put it another way. Can you have anything unless you are conscious of it? Can you eat a peach unless you are conscious of it? Can you drive your car unless you are conscious of it? Can you greet a friend unless you are conscious of something?

What did Jesus mean when He said *I am Alpha and Omega?* He meant that the whole Creative Process begins and ends in God. There is nothing before *Alpha*, and there is nothing after *Omega*. This is the whole operation; this is the way the Law works. I AM A AND Z. The A of Life is consciousness, awareness; the Z is demonstration.

Put Imagination to Work.—Jesus gave us another wonderful concept. Whatever you can imagine is yours, and you cannot demonstrate anything on the material plane that you cannot imagine first. *And all things, what so ever ye shall ask, believing, ye shall receive.* Now ponder that statement for a few moments and make sure that you understand it. Creative imagination is a Divine Faculty given to every man. You have it now. When you put it to work, it opens your consciousness.

"But that is ridiculous," someone says. "Imagination is fantasy. It is a waste of time." Do you know that you can't imagine anything that doesn't have a basis in fact? Even your wildest and sometimes horrible imaginings result from putting together parts of things you have seen or read or heard about. You say, "I want a better position," "I want a new house," "I want more friends," "I want to travel," "I want a larger income." You know that each of these things has a factual basis. Then meet the test. Answer the question: Can you imagine it?

Do you know that *I and the Father are one?* Do you know God AS YOU? Do you have acceptance? Do you have self-completeness? If you have, what you want is yours. You have taken it into consciousness; it exists for you. It objectifies as you.

It is you. If you can imagine it, you can have it. If you cannot imagine it, you cannot have it. That is the Law. *Whatsoever things you desire when you pray, believe that ye have received them and ye shall have them.*

You say, "I want a farm of my own," "I want to be a great chemist (engineer, minister, leader, surgeon)." Why not? The desire is spiritually legal—that is, it harms no one. The wish is already established. That which you wish to be IS. The Kingdom of Heaven is finished. God's work is already done. You *are* that which you wish yourself to be right now. Then why are you looking inside instead of out? Why are you wishing instead of being? Is it because you have something else mixed up in your picture?

Do you also say, "I am too old," "I am too poor," "I do not have enough education"? But the power is right there. It is within you. You could not have a desire that is not already established in God, one that is not awaiting your faith to be objectified. The farm is within you. The engineer is within you. The minister is within you. The chemist is within you.

But you have to imagine it, believe it, feel it, embody it, dream it, become it.

The Everlasting Now.—There is no time in Spirit. *The fields are already white unto harvest.* The Kingdom of Heaven is at hand. But there must be immediacy in your prayer. That promotion, that new refrigerator, that trip to Hawaii, that thing you are seeking to demonstrate—if imagination says "next year," consciousness says "next year" and God says "next year." But Jesus says, *Thy kingdom come in earth as it is in heaven.* Note that IS. *Behold, now is the accepted time; behold, now is the day of salvation.* The time of God's giving is always NOW.

Does anything happen when you pray? Does your word have power? Is it backed by faith and acceptance? Do you accept your good with every cell in your body? Do you feel it clear down to the tips of your toes? What is the *word* that the metaphysician talks so much about? It is thought. *In the beginning was the Word, and the Word was with God, and the Word was God... And the Word was made—flesh.*

Do you see what we are talking about? This word you speak in the consciousness that you are One with the Father is not a word of the head but a word of the heart. It is the word of God. It is God. *Speak the word only and my servant shall be healed.* The word which is to be spoken into manifestation is a part of the whole. It is spoken with the understanding that *I and the Father are one.*

Tell me, then, about your word. Do you take it into consciousness? Do you speak as one having authority? Do you believe that the desire is fulfilled before you speak or do you only hope that it is? When does the word become God? When you can say, *I and the Father are one.*

If you will go back and study the above paragraph carefully you will see that what we been talking about is Consciousness. In the beginning was Consciousness—and the Consciousness was with God—and the Conciousness was God—and the Consciousness became flesh. The power of the word is in the faith and consciousness back of it. *The words that I speak unto you, they are spirit and they are life... So shall my word be...; it shall not return unto me void, but it shall accomplish that which I please.* The accomplishing word is not only the spirit filled word but the believing word. It is both the *substance of things hoped for and the evidence of things not seen.*

If ye have faith [awareness and acceptance] *and doubt not... ye shall say unto this mountain, Be thou removed and be thou cast into the sea; it shall be done.* Note the words, *ye shall say.* Who is it that is going to speak the word that will cast this mountain of trouble into the sea? Why YOU, of course. You are the one who will speak this mountain out of existence. *Ye shall say* means you who are reading this book.

You Determine the Level of Your Consciousness.—Look at your consciousness for a moment. What do you find there? Which side of the fence are you on? What are you seeing? What are you feeling? What are you thinking? What are you accepting? Something evil? Something partial? Something poor? Something sick? Something feeble? Well, whatever it is, that is what you will get and what you will continue to get until you want something else.

Just what are you seeking? What is it that you are trying to do? What is it that you want to be? Is it necessary for your fulfillment? Will it add to your peace? Can you imagine it? Look again and tell me: Is it complete and finished in your thought?

Then speak your word and take the thing you seek. Don't muff it by fears and challenges. Don't strain. Don't doubt. Don't throw obstacles in the way. Just take it by faith. *If thou canst believe, all things are possible to him that believeth.* This is not the head belief of mental assent but the heart belief of faith and trust.

Are you seeking that state of mind by which the things desired become the things possessed? Then you must come by the way of Jesus' appointing. *Seek ye first the kingdom of God* [the Consciousness of ALL-NESS]. Recognize your Oneness with it. Unite your mind with His Mind. Claim your Good.

There is an old fable about a dog that boasted of his ability as a runner. One day he gave chase to a rabbit but failed to catch it. The other dogs ridiculed him on account of his previous boasting. His reply was, "You must remember that the rabbit was running for his life; I was only after my dinner." The incentive is all important. You now have the incentive. If you are seeking loaves and fishes, you will not put the same quality of consciousness into your search that you will if your ambition is deeper and more serious. Seeking the Spirit back of things not only puts you in possession of things but enables you to use them freely. It is the one thing that cannot be lost, stolen, fluctuate, or fail.

Emerson said, "What a man does, that he has. What has he to do with hope or fear? In himself is his might. Let him regard no good as solid but that which is in his nature and which must grow out of him as long as he exists. The goods of fortune may come and go like summer leaves; let him scatter them on every wind as the momentary signs of his productiveness."

Knock, and it shall be opened unto you.—Are your knuckles raw from knocking? Are your eyes tired from seeking? Are your vocal chords parched from asking? You set out to demonstrate health. You observe all the laws. You pray and treat. But nothing happens. Perhaps you knock at the door for supply. Your need is desperate. The mortgage is due, and the creditors are breathing down your neck.

But no one opens the door. What are you going to do? Pin crape on your sleeve and bemoan your fate? Are you going to become cynical, frustrated and embittered? Are you going to settle back in your defeat, shrug your shoulders and say, "What's the use?" Are you going to run up the flag of surrender and say bitterly, "It doesn't work for me," or more bitterly, "It doesn't work"?

The thing to do is to recognize that closed doors come to all alike. It doesn't make any difference how good you are or how much you know, sooner or later you will come to doors that do not open. You will resist them or you will use them, according to your attitude toward them. If you see them as dead ends, you will go down under the belief. If you ask, "Why?" and find the cause to be your own divided mind, your lack of realization, you can make the necessary change within yourself and knock again. If you see them as tests of your faith, you will continue to knock.

Did Peter become panicky, fearful, or hysterical when the door did not open? Did he fly into a rage? What do the Scriptures say? *Peter continued knocking.* What a lesson in that for us! Our faith is tested by our ability, *having done all to stand.* It is tested by our ability to keep knocking. Closed doors are often simply a series of questions concerning our fortitude and our stability; they are the measure of our faith.

Can you be patient in the face of delay? Can you be positive in the face of negation? Can you be dauntless in the face of defeat? Can you be confident in the face of ruin? Can you be peaceful in the midst of confusion? Can you maintain your faith in the midst of doubt and uncertainty?

There is always the possibility that what you most desire is not the thing that you should have. Can you not look back in your life and see occasions when the thing that happened was far better than the thing you projected? A locked door may be side by side with one that is opened wide.

If you have a close relationship to God, it should be easy for you to trust everything in your life to Him. It should be as easy to give Him your problems, difficulties, and needs as it is to trust Him to develop the seeds which you plant in the ground or to regulate your heartbeats and the other involuntary processes of your body. *Of myself I can do nothing, but with God all things are possible.* All is *All-there-is.* You are a point of expressions for this Allness; but until you identify yourself with it, you are like an electric light globe with the switch turned off.

Why is the Consciousness of Oneness so important in spiritual demonstration? Because One with God is a majority. Walter Lanyon says, "When you become one with anything, you become that thing, so to speak; so to become one with law is actually to become that law in action."

Now ask yourself, "Am I the law of health in action? Am I the law of success in action? Am I the law of prosperity in action?" If your answer is *No*, ask yourself, "*Why not?*" The answer you will probably get is this: "You are trying to contact God from a point outside yourself." It is not by mouthing affirmations or singing hymns that God becomes a *very present help in trouble*; it is only by working from the Center out, only by becoming the Law in action.

What must one do after he has impressed his desire on the subconscious mind? He must trust God for the perfect outworking of the Law. What does God ask of us? Just one thing—faith.

Why do we complicate the process? Is it wholly because we cannot believe that results will come from simply trusting? Isn't our real trouble that we cannot quite let go? What does it mean to let go? It means to close the bulkhead doors so tightly that they cannot be opened, to put our claim in an airtight compartment that we no longer have access to, to go all the way in trusting Him, and not to go back to the problem in thought until it is solved.

Is there anything so hard about that? Not any more so than dropping a piece of paper in the waste basket and leaving it there.

You let go of your needs and wants, your ambitions and aspirations, your fears and your worries, your obligations and your responsibilities, your claims and your desires in perfect trust and abandonment, knowing that GOD TAKES HOLD WHEN YOU LET GO.

If you take them up in thought again after placing them lovingly in His hands, you only delay His action. You must trust them to Him with the same abandon that you drop a seed into the ground. Jesus said that the seed must rot before the new shoot can come forth. It cannot rot, however, if you keep digging it up.

Do you see how stupid it is to try to force God to do your bidding and how wise it is to let Him express Himself through you AS YOU? Do you want the peace and rest that come through spiritual relaxation? Then take your place in the consciousness of Christ. Identify yourself with the Isness of your Divine Self.

Clothe yourself in faith, trust, assurance, receptivity, and gratitude and then beat upon the gates of Heaven with all the indomitability, importunity, persistence, and spiritual strength which you have. The secret of successful achievement is to press your claim persistently and consistently.

Do you understand the difference between instantaneous healing and gradual healing? It is the difference between absolute acceptance and partial acceptance. Instantaneous healing comes when you are able to accommodate the idea with which you have become One. A thing is true because IT IS TRUE. You do not have to make it so.

"Blind faith," someone has said, "follows God's Laws ignorantly and haphazardly and with intermittent results. Understanding faith works with God's Laws harmoniously and successfully." Prayer made in understanding faith exerts a powerful influence.

When you have absolute faith, it will be as easy to heal a cancer as a headache. Do you believe that you are going to get the things you have asked for? Do you feel it in every atom of your being? Do you realize it in your mind? *Believe that ye receive them and ye shall have them.* In other words, accept your fulfilled desire in your whole consciousness, *nothing doubting.*

"Assume a Virtue, If You Have It Not."—Dramatize your affirmation, if need be. Pretend to yourself that the desired condition is already established. Live, think, act, and speak as though it were fulfilled now. *If all things are possible to him that believeth,* the belief must come first. Even though you are terrified by the thing that has happened to you, you must keep your mental level high.

Put on the whole armor of God. Call upon your dynamic and creative faith. Apply it to your problem. Tell God that your faith in His Power is limitless and that you are calling upon that Power now. Realize that the subconscious receives your directions and acts upon them immediately. *If God be for us* [for me], *who can be against us* [against me]? Repeat this statement many times. Get your consciousness of Oneness and partnership with God, and nothing can defeat you.

With every demonstration you make, your faith will be nourished, vitalized, and strengthened. You will come eventually to the place at which you will make your demonstrations easily and naturally. You will build up within your consciousness a magnetic field which will attract all the elements and factors needed for your success.

Why do you sit still?—There are factors that delay healing and other answers to prayer. Through your objective mind, you can identify these, reason about them and analyze yourself to see which of them are operating in your life. By putting your faith to work through your knowledge of how to use your subjective mind (which is one with the Creative Mind of God), you can eliminate them.

Doubt not.—Doubt is one of the malignant forces that attempt to operate against faith.

If ye have faith and doubt not... whatsoever things ye shall ask in prayer, believing, ye shall receive... Whosoever... shall not doubt in his heart, but shall believe that those things which he saith shall come to pass; he shall have whatsoever he saith.

We open the mind through faith and close it through doubt. *A kingdom divided against itself shall fall.* The ancient plea, *Lord, I believe; help thou mine unbelief,* is made by each one of us at some time, for the objective mind registering the impressions of the senses challenges the *substance of things hoped for, the evidence of things not seen.*

A very ardent young lover began his letter to his fiancée in this way:

"Darling, I'd swim rivers and seas to be near you. I'd climb all the mountain ranges in the world to be at your side."

But after pages and pages of sentiment he added this postscript:

"I'll see you Sunday night if it doesn't rain."

So it is with us. We say, "I would do anything to get more faith," "I'd give my right arm to learn how to pray." But there is always the postscript, "I'll take up the study in earnest if I can find the time," "I'll take the course if it doesn't cost too much." *If it doesn't rain, if it doesn't inconvenience me, if I can spare the money.* The *if* betrays the divided mind. St. James said, *A double-minded man is unstable in all his ways.*

Dean Inge once said, "We are losing our Christianity not because anyone is taking it from us, but because it is a religion for heroes, and we are merely harmless, good natured, little people who want to have a good time."

What does the Law say? *He that loseth his life shall find it... And ye shall serve the Lord your God, and he shall bless thy bread and water; and I will take sickness away from the midst of thee... Seek ye first the kingdom of God and his righteousness and all these things shall be added unto you... Trust in the Lord and do good... and verily thou shalt be fed.*

Only by continual discipline and practice can we become single-minded, one-pointed. Our watch word must be *Emmanuel... God with us.*

"Think of self, trouble grows; Think of God, trouble goes."

Your Father knoweth that ye have need of all these things.— Outlining the process by which the aid we seek will come is another factor in delay. We say, *In thee is my trust,* and then we tell Him how to do His work.

Are you still outlining when you pray? Are you still trying to figure out when and how the prayer will be answered? Turn on your trust. Let go some more and keep letting go until the problem is completely out of your hands. The when is not important; there is no time in Heaven but now. All you need to do is to follow the rules:

1. *Ask.*
2. If there is no answer, *Seek.*
3. If you still get no answer, *Knock.*

Put all the possibilities, probabilities, chances and likelihoods out of your mind and give God a free hand to help you in His way. Outlining is trying to get God to go your way.

My thoughts are not your thoughts, neither are my ways your ways. For as the heavens are higher than the earth, so are my ways and my thoughts higher than yours... Eye hath not seen, nor ear heard, neither have entered into the heart of man, the things which God hath prepared for them that love him.

Be sure you understand the principle involved. Let us assume that you are in need of financial help and that you are starting out to demonstrate supply metaphysically. How do you go about it? The first thing you do is to make your claim by impressing it with deep feeling upon the subconscious mind. You assume the attitude that would be yours if the desire had already materialized. You declare your Oneness with God's Allness, and you take the words of Jesus personally, *Son, thou art ever with me and all that I have is thine.*

You believe this promise and you accept it for yourself. Your mind is now open to the things of God, and you are ready to take the final steps. There are three of them:

1. You call upon your creative imagination to help you see in your mind the thing you want.

2. You feel God's power entering your treatment and accomplishing what you have asked for.
3. You claim fulfillment of your desire by saying, "In the name of the Father, and of the Son, and of the Holy Ghost. Amen."

Finally, you rest the case with Him in perfect trust. You know that if God cannot do it, it cannot be done. The word, *Amen*, which means *so it is or so be it*, is your recognition of the fact that God has already done everything that needs to be done, that you are already that which you want to be, that you already have that which you seek.

Are you ready to take the final step, or are you still wondering how your need for more money will be met? Perhaps several possibilities run through your mind: "Frank owes me money. Maybe he will pay me." "It's a long time since I had a raise. I could ask for one tomorrow." "Possibly someone will buy those lots." "Perhaps someone will leave me some money." "Maybe it isn't God's will that I should have this demonstration."

The Law says that God can't take hold until you let go. Put all these possibilities out of your mind and think only of God's power and His willingness to use it in your behalf. He has ways of fulfilling your desires which you have not even thought of. Cling to that trust. Increase your understanding of it. Be true to it. Dare to leave everything quietly to God. Dare to claim His overflowing abundance in the midst of poverty and lack. Dare to trust Him through every difficulty and every vicissitude. Dare to claim that God can do, that God will do, that God is doing whatever is necessary right now. Dare to acknowledge the Presence and Power of God in every person, circumstance, condition, and thing. Know God in yourself AS YOU.

Do you feel the thrill and upsurge of power that comes to you as you say these words—God in Me AS ME?

It is I, be not afraid.—Fear, which is faith in negative, is an agent of doubt and often the cause of it. It is faith misdirected. It is faith in evil.

God didn't plant failure, limitation, trouble, worry, fear and disease in you. You thought them up yourself, fed them with your thought and attention, kept them alive with your belief and so continued to attract them to your experience. How, then, do you expect Him to answer your prayers? How can He get through a mind choked with negation? You cannot claim the blessing until you make room for it, until you identify yourself with it. The mind can think only one thought at a time; the sooner you give up your negations the better. The Law is infallible, immutable, and inexorable. There is no evading It. It works for you only as you bring yourself into obedience to It. To receive directly from God, you must let go of everything unlike Him. Only then does *all that the Father hath* become yours.

Here is a middle-aged man who is in a desperate situation financially. He asks for spiritual help and then explains all the reasons why he cannot get ahead.

"The cards are stacked against me," he says. "I have tried to find a job but no one wants a man over fifty. There are no opportunities for a man my age. There is no work in the town where I live and I have no money to go elsewhere. What good would it do anyway because the list of unemployed is growing everywhere? I am really not well enough to take a job if it were offered to me."

This sounds like an exaggeration but such a case is common. This man tells his practitioner that he is looking to God for supply and then enumerates all the reasons why He cannot succeed in giving it to him.

Why is such a man sick and poverty-stricken? Because he is misdirecting his faith. He is directing it into negative channels instead of positive channels. He is looking to God and looking away from Him at the same time. He does not know that it takes the same power to go forward as it does to go backward. Will his prayers be answered? Yes, in terms of more lack. Why? Because he is giving more power to his circumstances than he is to God. How can he change the action of the Law? How can he cause It to work for him instead of against him? He can do it by changing his relationship to It.

This man reminds us of the disciples when the listening multitude needed to be fed. They were overwhelmed by the problem. Can't you hear them?

"We have here," they said, "but five loaves and two small fishes."

"My goodness! Is that all we have?"

"Are you sure? Don't we have anything else?"

"That is all there is."

"Just five loaves and two measly fish! And five thousand hungry persons!"

"Let's tell Jesus to send them to the village to buy food. Of course, this is a desert place and it's already getting dark. But let's all go together and tell Him what we think. We must save our faces."

Now listen to Jesus: *They need not depart: give ye them to eat.*

You remember the end of the story. *He blessed, and brake, and gave the loaves to his disciples, and the disciples to the multitude. And they all did eat and were filled: and they took up of the fragments that remained twelve baskets full.*

You and I often face the five-loaf-and-two-fish problem. We too tend to overstate our poverty and thereby increase it. Yes, like the disciples, forget how close we are to the Source of Supply, how near He is who came that we *might have life and have it more abundantly.*

It is one thing to affirm the Allness-of-God and another thing to make a connection with it. *All that the Father hath is mine* only when I am in His consciousness, only when I have the conviction that it is already mine.

Jesus knew that the Law of Faith works negatively as well as positively. When a man says, "There are no opportunities for one my age. Nobody wants a man over fifty. The cards are stacked against me. I never get the breaks. I am not well enough to take a job," and he believes, that... *which he saith* [accepts it as true], *shall come to pass.* What he believes will continue to manifest in his affairs. God is not unkind or unfriendly, but He works through Law. Life responds to us by corresponding to our states of thought. It gives to us according to our expectations. The Law is impersonal. It works the way we use It.

Ye have not received the spirit of bondage again to fear.— Bondage to the past that continues to be an active force in our thought and feeling and action can be escaped from only by accepting the promise. *Ye shall know the truth, and the truth shall make you free.*

The subjective mind is the seat of the memory. Buried deep in it are the causes of much of the delay we experience in appropriating our good. These unseen and forgotten forces tend to keep us in a state of restlessness and frustration.

To all outward appearances there may be nothing in your life that is contrary to the Law of God. But you are troubled much of the time, uncertain, vague, jumpy and haunted by fears you cannot even name.

Do I hear you say that this does not apply to you? Then you are an exception to the rule. Either that, or you have not honestly faced your delays, disappointments and defeats. Have you ever desired something which despite all your best efforts has eluded you? Have you ever entered one of those hectic periods when everything goes wrong and nothing goes right? Most of us have suffered frustrations and disappointments and some of us have dwelt upon them until they have taken root.

Are you asking such questions as these: What is this imperious voice which speaks out of the shadows and says *no* when it should say *yes*? Why is my healing so long delayed? Why do my goals elude me? Why this mental and spiritual conflict within me? How long must I continue half-slave and half-free?

Do you really want to know? Do you really mean to do something about it? Then listen to Jesus: *Ye cannot serve God and mammon.* You cannot follow two lines of thought and get one result. You will continue half-slave and half-free until you cleanse the mind and flush out every old fixed unhappy thought that enslaves you.

You may not recall when you first entered this unhappy state, but there is One in you that knows. There is One who has provided a way out. There is One who can make you wholly free, One who says, *Come unto me all ye who are weary and heavy laden and I will give you rest.*

Suppressed desires, forced inhibitions, race beliefs in such things as heredity and predestination, forgotten experiences that left remorse, resentment, hatred, jealousy, envy in their wake often prove to be the unknown forces that play upon our lives and express themselves in our experience. Sometimes they are consciously accepted but most often they lie deeply buried in the subconscious mind but not dead. Accepted, they make wonderful alibis for shortcomings.

Have you ever heard anyone say such things as these? "That's the way I was brought up. I can't change now." "My father was tubercular and so I have never been strong." "Of course, I'm afraid of lightning. When I was a child, mother used to send me under the bed." "I forgave her, but I didn't forget and I just can't stand her." "Oh, we'll always be poor. We always have been."

If you have any doubt about the effect of these fixed and unhappy thoughts that afflict most of humanity, observe their patterns in the lives of individuals. Observe the effect upon the eyes, the face, the skin, the pulse, the manner of speaking, acting and thinking. Anything in the subconscious mind that lowers the mental level lowers the vitality and drags down the health.

Dr. Frank J. Sladen of the Ford Hospital in Detroit, Michigan says, "I maintain that a man cannot live without Christ unless he admits that living in unhappiness and conflict, in hate, envy, selfishness, futility, nervousness and fatigue, in slavery to innumerable possibilities of compensatory and destructive habits is really living.

"In my eyes, people come figuratively limping into church, handicapped and sick from living with unsolved problems within their own bodies, or their homes, or with their children, business or other relationships. Even if they don't realize it and don't consider themselves ill, they do resemble—going to and from church—our patients as they go to and from the office; except that the former wear their best Sunday clothes."

Many people try to demonstrate Truth while still filled with untruth. It doesn't work. Many people have accepted Christ in the conscious mind but not in the subconscious and here much of our conversion falls down. When the dentist pulls an offending tooth, he knows that he must get the root or it will set up an infection that will poison the whole system later on. So it is with these habit patterns of the past. Until the roots are withdrawn, the manifestation of faith will be delayed.

These habit patterns that cause us to limp through life may have started as some little sin, fear, mistake or imagined hurt. As they were repeated, they gradually cut a pattern in the subconscious mind and all our thoughts from then on flowed through this pattern. Some of them got roots through repetition and others through repression or suppression. We dwelt on them so long that they sank into the subconscious and there formed a center of their own from which, without our consent, they exert a constant power. To a greater or less degree, we all have these unconscious influences in our lives, and fight them as we may, as long as the roots are there, our thought is drained through them.

There is a way to root out all these habit patterns of the past but it cannot be effective until the cause of the trouble is known. By that I mean that we cannot apply a constructive course of action until the offending pattern has been unmasked.

The first step, therefore, is to find this hidden memory pattern and to bring it out into the light. Where does your trouble come from? When did it start? What caused you to be so fearful? When did you first get angry? Who was it that hurt you and why? Why were you resentful? Why were you disillusioned? What did you do that caused you to be ashamed? Why do you feel guilty? Try to recall. Get very still and try to remember.

Command the subconscious mind to bring all these memories up to the conscious mind. Do it in the same way that you recall a name, date or event. Make your demand and then turn your thought to something else. Whatever information you are seeking will come forth. Does not the Bible say that *There is nothing covered that shall not be revealed; and hid, that shall not be known?* The answer may come while you are in the Silence or it may come while you are thinking about something else, but come it will. *In the moment ye think not, the Son of man cometh.*

The next step is to replace the offending pattern that you have uncovered with one that is so strongly positive that it literally reverses the negative one. Let us suppose that the offending thought pattern is fear—fear of any one of the thousands of things that hold people in bondage.

To reverse fear, enter the Silence and meditate upon a statement of truth such as this: MY FAITH IN GOD DELIVERS ME FROM ALL FEAR. Impress these words upon the subconscious mind with deep feeling until a great sense of peace (which is the answer) comes over you. Then speak to your subconscious mind in some such manner as this:

> SUBCONSCIOUS MIND OF ME, YOU ARE A VIBRANT LIVING PART OF ME.
>
> YOU ARE INSTANTLY RECEPTIVE AND RESPONSIVE TO MY CALL. YOU ALWAYS OBEY MY COMMANDS AND DIRECTIONS. YOU FULFILL MY DESIRES TO THE LETTER. YOU ALWAYS DO WHAT I WANT DONE.
>
> THERE IS NOTHING THAT YOU CANNOT DO. I HAVE ABSOLUTE FAITH IN YOU BECAUSE YOU ALWAYS ACT UPON THOSE IDEAS WHICH I FEEL TO BE TRUE.
>
> YOU ARE ALWAYS WAITING FOR MY CALL, AND RIGHT NOW I WANT YOU TO REVERSE THIS PATTERN OF FEAR WITH A PATTERN OF FAITH. ELIMINATE FROM MY MIND ALL FEAR AND ALL BELIEF THAT ANYTHING IS NOW WRONG OR EVER CAN BE WRONG.
>
> INSULATE MY MIND AGAINST FEAR SO THAT NO THOUGHT OF FEAR CAN EVER

ENTER MY CONSCIOUSNESS AGAIN. YOU CAN DRAW THE ROOTS OF THIS OLD FEAR OUT OF ME AND I KNOW THAT YOU ARE DOING IT NOW. GO ALL THE WAY BACK TO MY MEMORIES AND HEAL ALL THESE THINGS THAT HAPPENED IN THE PAST SO THAT THEY WILL NOT TROUBLE ME ANY MORE. YOU HAVE RECEIVED MY INSTRUCTIONS AND YOU HAVE RESPONDED TO MY CALL. YOU HAVE BROKEN THE CHAINS WHICH HAVE BOUND ME.

I FEEL THE FULLNESS OF PERFECT FAITH IN EVERY ATOM OF MY BEING. MY FAITH IN YOUR POWER IS UNLIMITED AND I KNOW THAT THE HEALING FREEING WORK BEGUN IN ME WILL CONTINUE UNTIL I AM EVERY WAY WHOLE.

Such a meditation may be used for any intention simply by changing the words to correspond to the nature of your desire.

Judge Troward said, "Whatever we believe, does, for us, in very fact exist." That is true about these unconscious forces which, unchallenged, plague the mind and life. If you have a root pattern of fear, if you believe that the cause of your fear is real, it will be real to you. It will injure you quite as much as though it were real.

Therefore, change your consciousness from the negative pattern into the positive pattern. You must come to see that these doubts that darken your vision, these fears that paralyze your efforts, these ghosts that haunt you, these memories of people who represent opposition are really nothing more nor less than your own reactions to the things that have happened to you. They have power only because you give it to them. Withdraw the power by reversing the pattern, and they will cease to trouble you.

When you have cleansed your mind and brought it around to a normal, natural state, you will be able to say with Jesus, *The prince of this world cometh and findeth nothing in me* [nothing for evil to act with]. When the stream of consciousness is no longer diluted with doubts, fears, inhibitions, and repressions, faith has an open channel through which to flow. Energies will be quickened, resolution strengthened, confidence deepened, life broadened and enriched, and courage made sublime.

Several years ago, a prominent woman called to ask if I would come and pray with her for healing. She had a broken hip that would not heal, and I soon found in talking with her that the delayed healing was not in the hip itself. The doctor who had been called to set the hip after the accident had made a mistake and another doctor had to be called six months later to set the hip properly. X-ray pictures showed that the hip was then set perfectly but still it did not heal.

In questioning the woman further, I found that her heart was filled with bitterness and hatred toward the doctor who had made the mistake. Her body was now filled with great pain and suffering.

"I must have relief," she said. "I believe that God can heal me."

"He can heal you," I replied, "if you give up this hatred, but He can't heal you so long as you are generating this poison in your mind." "Well, there is nothing I can do about that," she answered, "for I shall hate that doctor as long as I live."

"Very well," I replied. "Then there is nothing I can do for you."

Several months elapsed and the woman called again. This time I found her in a very different frame of mind. "I have been thinking," she said, "about what you told me the last time you were here and I have decided to try to love Dr.—. I want you to pray for me that I may be forgiven for the hatred I have been holding toward him."

God had touched this woman's heart and she saw for the first time that her faith in God's power could not operate in the presence of her resentment, that love and hatred could not dwell in the same place at the same time, and that without love there would be no healing. There was now a deep desire in her heart to be liberated from the feeling of bitterness and hatred which had been filling her body with pain. She was ready for Christ to come in and break the chains of torment which she had bound around herself. She was freed and her body was healed.

Take Three Steps: Turn, Deny, Realize.—I like *The Treatment Book* written by F. L. Rawlson many years ago. In it, he says, "Turn in thought at once to Heaven."

Turning one's thought is the first step. He was saying practically what Jesus said, *Thy kingdom come. Thy will be done, in earth* [here, now, in you, in John, in Mary] *as it is* [being done] *in heaven.* Any disease there? NO! Any sudden death there?

No death at all. Any cancer there? No! Having gotten the realization of the Heaven within you, pray for yourself or another, knowing that His will is that we be perfect here and now even as He is perfect.

Rawlson said secondly, "Deny the existence in Heaven of the wrong thing thought of, seen, or felt."

You are praying for someone with cancer. Do you see what a boon it is to be able to say, "There is no such thing in heaven. Heaven is within me and I am within heaven"? And then to say, "*Oh, God, Thy will be done, in earth* [here in me, or here in my friend] *as it is in heaven*"?

"Thirdly," Rawlson urges, "realize the existence of the opposite."

When we hold with sufficient tenacity to the Truth, that is, to the Reality of the Spiritual Plane, we get grace from above to change conditions on the physical plane.

The most powerful treatment you can get is the realization of the truth in the statement, *I and the Father are one*. There is nothing more powerful than the Consciousness of Oneness with God.

As I write to you today, it is snowing. There is no argument about it. When you picked up this book to study, there wasn't anything in you that doubted it was a book. When you can say to a person with cancer, "You haven't any cancer," with the same conviction and realization that you say, "This is a book," there will be no cancer.

Man made the devil to oppose God, sickness to oppose health, poverty to oppose prosperity, hell to oppose Heaven by his ignorance or his refusal to recognize and realize his Oneness with God. But no matter how long he has been in the desert of duality, no matter how he has messed things up, the moment he accepts his Oneness with the Father, he becomes *a new creature*. The thing he is seeking is the thing he will get when he believes that he has it. The signs follow them that believe.

Because God is, you are. The very fact that you exist is proof that you are some part of the Whole, and on this rests your faith. You know THAT YOU ARE. Are what? SPIRIT. When the Prodigal Son in his destitution said, *I will arise and go unto my father*, he went unto his own Consciousness—the Presence of the Whole. He said in substance, "I shall arise from these human limitations and regain my Consciousness of Oneness with the Father."

Through faith, you come to see that God is that Something within you that knows Itself. *The Lord thy God in the midst of thee is mighty.* When you demonstrate the Allness-of-God, you recognize that It cannot know anything other than Itself. It includes everything. It *is* everything. It cannot know anything separated from Itself.

As you turn to God, He turns toward you. *I shall arise and go unto my father.* Father of what? The Father of my body; the Father of my business; the Father of my work; the Father of everything in my world. Like the Prodigal Son, you effect this union for yourself. The Consciousness of the Presence is that state of mind which believes in the good, the enduring, and the true.

When you dare to arise and go to the Father's house, you arrive by the way of your Oneness with God. There is nothing in your mind to contradict this Oneness. You believe that your word is using a Power greater than Itself and that there is nothing in the Universe to deny it. You accept the invitation, *Call upon me*, knowing that every demand you make upon the Presence will be honored. The Presence has only one purpose and that is to experience Itself in you. You have only one purpose and that is to accept the Presence. When you return to the Father's House, you change from self-consciousness to God-Consciousness.

Why tarriest thou? arise.—Are you afraid to try your faith? Are you afraid that it won't work? Then dismiss such a foolish thought from your mind. Even while you are afraid that your faith won't work, it is working. It takes just as much faith to believe that faith doesn't work as to know that it does. *What doth it profit, my brethren, if a man say he hath faith, but hath not works? Can faith save him?...*

By works a man is justified and not by faith only... For as the body without the spirit is dead, so faith without works is dead also.

Are you still trying to force your good into manifestation by concentration, through breathing exercises, through formulas or other gimmicks? Be still and know that I am God. If you would avoid the tiresome treadmill of making demonstrations month after month, lose yourself in the One. *Leave all and follow me. Speak the word only and my servant shall be healed. Thou shalt also decree a thing and it shall be established unto thee.*

There stands the Truth towering like the Rock of Gibraltar above all your futile efforts! God in the midst of you! God AS YOU! Life AS YOU! Power AS YOU! Health AS YOU! Prosperity AS YOU!

Do you say, "If I had just had this teaching in my youth! If I could only have had it sooner!" Sooner than what? Don't you know that when the student is ready the teacher appears? The teacher is here. You are ready now. It is time to act. Do something. Put the Law to work. Take your stand. Hold to it through thick or thin. God works not by doing but by Being. He waits to express Himself AS YOU. Think of yourself as God in objective action. Think of Him in you AS YOU. *Know ye not that ye are the temple of the living God?*

Do you wish you had more faith? Are you waiting for it to develop before you make use of what you have? To increase the potential of faith, you must increase your expectations. You must as Jesus said, *Launch out into the deep.*

To become skillful in faith, you must practice faith. Imagination shows you the possibilities of God's Kingdom; faith makes them real.

Now is the accepted time.—Are you ready to put your faith to the test? Then get a pencil and paper and go to work. Put your prayer or treatment in words. See the problem, not as your imagination reports it but as it is in Truth. The answer awaits your application of the Law of Faith to bring it into manifestation. The orderly outworking of the Law follows as naturally as day follows night.

Apply the rule and the answer follows. What is the rule? *Seek ye first the Kingdom of God and His righteousness and all these things shall be added unto you.* In other words, put first things first. Seek first your conscious Oneness with God. *I and the Father are one.*

State as briefly as possible your intention—what you are seeking from God. Be very accurate and definite. Your formula (desire) must be just as clear and exact in your mind as if it were projected on a moving picture screen. Take these steps:

1. Release the desire with deep feeling to the subconscious mind.
2. Let God have it.
3. Don't question or wonder how the desire is going to be fulfilled. Dismiss any mental reservations or doubts.
4. Keep a positive image before your mind.
5. Accept the outcome of your prayer.

A claim upon Truth is an affirmation, and affirmations like rubber balls have a way of bouncing back. If results seem slow at first, take the intention into the Silence several times a day, impressing it with deep feeling upon the subconscious mind until you realize that the problem is already solved. Then loose it and let it go.

Remember that *A man can receive nothing, except it be given him from heaven*—from the Within. When you establish the consciousness of the Allness-of-God and your faith in Him is absolute, the words, *I and the Father are one*, will become so meaningful, so significant to you that there will be no doubt, no delay, no fear, no buried-but-not-dead malignant thought to repress or inhibit the freedom promised to you. *Ye shall know the truth and the truth shall make you free.*

Freedom from worry and anxiety releases your power to serve, develops appreciation of the beauty and magnitude of the world you live in, increases your joy in life.

Faith in God enables you to recognize that you are One with the Creative Principle which seeks constant expression through you. You realize that your responsibility is to release It through your acceptance as a channel through which the *Father's business* is carried on.

Freedom from the fears and anxieties commonly associated with the body comes from knowing there could be no physical manifestation of any kind if there were no Spiritual Cause.

Happily relating yourself to others becomes a matter of recognizing the perfect Spiritual Man in each individual you meet and in accepting your common Oneness of purpose.

Faith enables your first waking thought to be: *This is the day which the Lord hath made; we will rejoice and be glad in it.*

Are you ready to speak your word? Then lay the book down and close your eyes. Relax yourself into God's Presence body, mind, and spirit. Now hold the great desire of your heart in the forefront of consciousness for a moment. See it clearly. Get your sense of Oneness with God. Say with deep feeling: "THIS IS GOD WANTING WHAT I WANT THROUGH ME."

The companion book, *God Works Through Silence*, will be helpful to you at this point.

Questions and Answers about Faith

1. What is the Nature of Faith?

The nature of faith is to act; it acts not be· cause we make it act but because it is its nature to act. It is the governing factor in our activities. When faith is directed toward anything or anybody, it acts of its own volition. It draws to us that toward which our faith is directed.

2. What is the Overall Meaning of the Word Faith?

The general meaning of the word faith is a positive faith in God, the Good. It is a mental attitude which places God at the center of one's thoughts, words and acts. It means an absolute trust in and reliance upon God. Faith based upon Principle works when everything else fails.

3. What is Meant by A Living Faith?

A living faith is one that never doubts, falters or wavers. It clings to Divine Law until victory is realized. It not only believes but also accepts the fulfillment of every promise.

4. Why is Faith Called the Key to the Storehouse?

Faith is the causal factor in prayer. It accepts the unreasonable and believes the impossible. Someone has said, "Faith counts the things that are as though they were not, and the things that are not as though they were."

5. What is the Best Translation or Paul's Definition of Faith?

Moffatt's translation is the best rendering of this passage: Now faith means we are confident of what we hope for, convinced of what we do not see.

6. What is Required for an Irresistible Faith?

A consuming interest and a fixed desire are essential. The first is the driving power of faith; the second is the adhesive force which holds it to its goal. But desire and interest without faith are helpless.

7. Is Faith Intellectual or Spiritual?

Faith is essentially spiritual. It begins in the mind but comes to fruition in the heart. It is not measured by our intellectual ability to call a thing done, but by the realization in the heart that it is done.

8. What is the Difference between Faith and Belief?

Belief is of the intellect while faith is of the heart. Many people believe that they are one and the same thing, but that is not true. There is belief in faith, to be sure. But, as the Bible tells us, the devils also believe. Almost anyone can believe, but not everyone can exercise faith. Without the power of faith, belief is weak.

9. What is the Difference between Blind Faith and Understanding Faith?

Blind faith is an undeveloped faith. It follows God's laws ignorantly and haphazardly. Jesus spoke of the blind leading the blind. Understanding faith is a developed faith which works with God's laws harmoniously and successfully.

10. What is the Difference between Hope and Faith?

The best answer to this question is contained in an old, unaccredited quotation:

"Hope is a draft on futurity, sometimes honored but generally extended."

What does this tell you? Why is hope a draft on the future? Why is it generally extended? Because the future is a time apart from experience. Hope is honored only when it becomes faith. The difference is that between possibility and actuality. Hope is vague, uncertain, and sometimes forlorn while faith is definite, certain, and joyous. There is no delay in the answer to our prayers other than lack of faith.

11. Is it Necessary to have Faith in Yourself?

By all means, for faith in yourself, in your Real Self, is also faith in God. It is the starting point in every worthwhile accomplishment. If you do not have faith in Yourself, how can you have faith in God and in others? If you do not have faith in your ability, how can you put it to work? To be successful in any field of endeavor, you must not only have faith in God, but in Yourself and in others. According to your Self-confidence, be it done unto you. Believe you can and you will. If you follow and trust God's laws, you cannot fail. Know Yourself, believe in Yourself, think well of Yourself. Get rid of the worm-of-the-dust attitude. Self-confidence keeps the mind working at full speed and capacity and draws continuously upon the deeper resources within.

12. What is Meant by Negative Faith?

Fear is negative faith. Before we can fear anything, we must first have faith in it.

In fact, there can be no fear without faith. Fear is faith in evil.

13. What is most Important in Faith?

The most important thing in faith is its polarity. If your faith is positive, your thoughts will be positive, your words will be positive, and you will attract the best of everything. If your faith is negative, your thoughts will be negative, your words will be negative and you will attract the worst of everything. The polarity of your faith determines the results. If you have been living, thinking, acting, speaking on the negative side of life, the polarity of your faith needs changing.

14. What is meant by the Words, Polarity of Faith?

This is explained fully in Making The Contact, but I shall explain it briefly here. Faith is an attitude of the whole mind but fulfillment depends upon how deeply it is embedded in the subconscious. Out of the heart [subconscious mind] are the issues of life, said Jesus. No matter how much we may know intellectually, or how fervently we may pray, we always attract those things which we really are. The Law of Faith works both ways. If it is centered in the desirable, we attract the desirable. If it is centered in the undesirable, we attract the undesirable. That is the Law of Polarity.

15. How Does One Reverse Negative Polarity?

If faith is moving in the wrong direction, moving with a negative faith in evil, the only thing that needs to be done is to replace it with faith in good. Dr. C. O. Southard says, "Faith is not subject to argument or experiment. A person either believes or disbelieves; and since that faith is fixed in his subconscious, it can only be altered by the person himself, by his own efforts." Through the conscious mind, we analyze the character of our faith and make our decision. By using our will, we give attention to that which is good. What we give attention to becomes a moving force in our lives. Our faith in good expands and grows with use.

16. What Part Does the Subconscious Mind Play in Changing the Polarity of Faith?

The subconscious mind is the agent in changing the polarity of faith. First, you break up the negative habits of thought into which the subconscious has drifted by cleansing, by discipline, and by reversal. Then you condition it to hold the positive idea so firmly that it becomes the ruling factor in your thoughts, acts, and words. This can be done in meditation and in the Silence by impressing the idea with deep feeling upon the subconscious mind, not spasmodically but consistently.

You can accelerate the process by repeating the idea to yourself silently or aloud even as you go about your daily tasks: "My faith is in God, Omnipotent Good, as the only Presence and the only Power in me and in my affairs." As you do this, the old habit of thought will drop away and the new concept will take its place.

17. Why is Desire Necessary to the Perfect Outworking of Faith?

Desire is the matrix or mold through which faith works. It is the pattern through which demonstrations are made. Since the Law of Faith is impersonal and works for the bad as well as the good, and since we are continually believing in something, faith must have a guide. Whatsoever things ye desire when ye pray, believe that ye have received them and ye shall have them. When the desire is drawn out to a point (clearly defined), it becomes a demand. Our claim must be specific. We must have a vivid mental picture of what we want and here the imaginative faculty comes in. If you can imagine it, you can have it.

18. WHY Mvsr rm; Dnsnua BE FREED Barone IT CAN B12 FULFILLEDP

You might as well ask why the seed must be dropped into the ground before it can bring the increase. Seed cannot grow in your hand, on the shelf, or in the packet. Nor can your desire materialize if you hold it tightly in your thought. Jesus told us to Take no thought in order to give the desire a chance to go forth and bring back its reward.

Since the desire cannot be in two places at the same time, we must choose between fulfillment or frustration, between letting-go or holding-on. Jesus says that the seed must be dropped in the ground and that the desire must be relinquished to God. Take no thought does not mean lapsing into a state of unconsciousness; it means taking away the anxiety and fear which prevent the manifestation of your desire. When you release the desire in absolute forgetfulness, as Jesus did, the reward will come flowing into you in limitless measure. The way of fulfillment is not through thought but through God.

19. Why is Imagination Important in Spiritual Work?

Imagination stimulates the faculties of the mind. It expands consciousness and causes the mind to act along new lines. In metaphysics, we call it the great magnifier. If you are seeking to demonstrate a new home, you first decide what kind of a home you want. You see it so clearly in mind and in such detail that it is ever in the forefront of consciousness. Then you proceed to desire that home with all the passion and power of your soul.

The next step is to imagine yourself living in that home, moving from room to room with the members of your family and looking after it. This is the pattern of your desire and you keep that pattern before your attention. You make it so complete and perfect that there will never be any occasion to change it.

Imagination calls forth the great or the small according to the directions which you give it. Therefore, you must always seek the best, or that which is in accord with your highest ideals.

You should never make provision in your thought for a compromise. If you have an ideal house in mind, stick to that ideal. Apply all the power of your desire in making your dream come true.

20. What Part Does Expectation Play in Faith?

Expectation is faith in action. It is the feeling of fulfillment that comes from conviction. When you ask God for something, you must expect to receive what you ask. Expectation that comes from conviction does not run around beating the air in anxiety and suspense like the bettor at the race track. It is calm, tranquil and confident. Knowing that the desire is already fulfilled, it is quiet, serene and undisturbed. The expectation that gets phenomenal results wastes no time in speculation or doubt but accepts the promises of God as real and true. The more you expect, the harder your faith will work and the more it will accomplish. Expect the best, and you will get the best. Expect your faith to work, and it will work.

Expectation is not only a great stimulus to action but is also the push and motive power behind faith. It causes your faith to move with greater rapidity and power toward the fulfillment of your desire. Have you decided what you want? Then charge your mind with tremendous faith, interest and expectation. Know that your faith will produce it. Let your feeling of expectation be full, deep, and continuous.

21. What Part Does Concentration Play in Faith?

It is a mental law that any idea held firmly in the mind expresses itself in the body and affairs. But the only ideas that can be held firmly in the mind are those in which we have faith. The purpose of concentration in faith is to direct all our thoughts, feelings, and activities toward the fulfillment of our desire; in other words, to pinpoint the desire until it has been realized.

22. Why is Persistency Necessary to Success?

Persistency in faith is like fire under the boiler. It generates the energy necessary to success. There is nothing that cannot be accomplished through faith. But the trouble with most persons is that they do not hold to their faith long enough to realize the fulfillment of their desire. They are up today and down tomorrow. Their faith works by fits and starts. They lack the stick-to-itiveness which brings success. St. James says of such a person: *He that wavereth is like a wave of the sea, driven with the wind and tossed. Let not that man think that he shall receive any thing of the Lord.* The Law says that if we want success we must have faith and persistency. The promise is that In due season we shall reap if we faint not. The faint heart cripples faith and limits its capacity for worthwhile achievement. You cannot lose if you hang on.

23. What Part Does the will. Play in Desire?

The will plays no part in desire. In fact, it's only purpose is to determine whether you will believe or not. Until the desire has been placed in God's hands and forgotten in absolute trust, you delay the manifestation which it is His purpose to bring to pass. We do not will things into being. We will only to initiate action and to start things going. We will to act, to go forward, to achieve, to do more, and to be more.

We can achieve only what we will to achieve.

We can do only what we will to do. Will does not control faith or mental action, but it does give impetus and push to it.

24. Why is it that Many Persons do not Realize their Ideals?

They have not learned to will to believe; they have not learned to think what they want to think. Instead of acting from their own spiritual centers, they act on the beliefs and suggestions of others. They follow borrowed ideas instead of their own, and their paths are strewn with incomplete and unfinished tasks.

The way to overcome this tendency to drift and wander is to stay put. When you have made up your mind, when you know that your desire is right and spiritually legal, do not allow anything to influence you or cause you to change your mind.

25. What Happens to Faith that is not Used?

The same thing that happens to the tires on an automobile that is not used. To keep the rubber flexible and resilient, the car must be used. So it is with faith. If it is not used, it becomes static and weak. It is like a pool of water that is not agitated; it lacks power. Just as our muscles develop through exercise, faith grows through use. The Law says, "Use or lose."

26. Is it true that Negative thought Acts with Greater Power and Rapidity than Positive Thought?

No, it is not; it only seems that way. The force of any thought whether negative or positive is always in direct ratio to our faith. If we have more faith in evil than in good, the results will be more negative than positive.

27. What are the Six Steps in Demonstration?

- The first step is to formulate our desire—to see it clearly in mind.
- The second step is to impress it with deep feeling upon the subconscious mind, to see ourselves accomplishing that thing.
- The third step is to exercise our faith by accepting the desire as fulfilled.
- The fourth step is to keep our feeling and thinking moving with our desire.
- The fifth step is to order our conversation might—to speak always in terms of expectancy and fulfillment.
- The sixth step is to carry our desire into action—to act as if it were already fulfilled.

OTHER BOOKS YOU MAY LIKE

- 1984 by George Orwell, ISBN: 9789380914947
- 12 Years a Slave by Solomon Northup, ISBN: 9789390492374
- A Passage to India by E.M. Forster, ISBN: 9789354990205
- A Room of One's Own by Virginia Woolf, ISBN: 9789354990281
- A Streetcar Named Desire by Tennessee Williams, ISBN: 9788194748601
- A Wrinkle in Time by Madeleine L'Engle, ISBN: 9789354991066
- Abraham Lincoln by Lord Charnwood, ISBN: 9789380914251
- Animal Farm by George Orwell, ISBN: 9789380914701
- Annihilation of Caste by Dr B.R. Ambedkar, ISBN: 9789390492732
- Anthem by Ayn Rand, ISBN: 9789389157079
- As a Man Thinketh by James Allen, ISBN: 9788180320262
- As I Lay Dying by William Faulkner, ISBN: 9789390492381
- Believe in Yourself by Joseph Murphy, ISBN: 9789388118385
- Chanakya Neeti by Chanakya, ISBN: 9789389716276
- Civilization and Its Discontents by Sigmund Freud, ISBN: 9789387669499
- Demian by Hermann Hesse, ISBN: 9789387669567
- George Orwell Combo : Animal Farm & 1984, ISBN: 9789390492459
- Gravity by George Gamow, ISBN: 9789388118484
- Guerrilla Warfare by Ernesto Che Guevara, ISBN: 9789354990366
- How I Made $2,000,000 in the Stock Market by N. Darvas, ISBN: 9789389716283
- How to Attract Money by Joseph Murphy, ISBN: 9789388118408
- How to Develop Self Confidence by Dale Carnegie, ISBN: 9789387669000
- How to Enjoy Your Life and Your Job by Dale Carnegie, ISBN: 9789387669017
- How to Stop Worrying and Start Living by Dale Carnegie, ISBN: 9789380914817
- How to Win Friends and Influence People by D. Carnegie, ISBN: 9788180320217
- Jail Diary and Other Writings by Bhagat Singh, ISBN: 9789390492398

Develop your reading habit | **Gift books to your friends**

OTHER BOOKS YOU MAY LIKE

- Know Your Worth by NK Sondhi & Vibha Malhotra, ISBN: 9788180320231
- Lost Horizon by James Hilton, ISBN: 9789389716313
- Maneaters of Kumaon by Jim Corbett, ISBN: 9789354990731
- Mansarover 1 (Hindi) by Premchand, ISBN: 9789380914978
- Mansarover 2 (Hindi) by Premchand, ISBN: 9789380914985
- Meditation and Its Methods by Swami Vivekananda, ISBN: 9789389716320
- Meditations by Marcus Aurelius, ISBN: 9789388118736
- My Experiments with Truth by Mahatma Gandhi, ISBN: 9789387669291
- My Inventions: The Autobiography of Nikola Tesla, ISBN: 9789388118132
- One, None and a Hundred Thousand by Luigi Pirandello, ISBN: 9789389716337
- Relativity by Albert Einstein, ISBN: 9789380914220
- Reminiscences of a Stock Operator by Edwin Lefevre, ISBN: 9788194764816
- Scientific Healing Affirmations by P. Yogananda, ISBN: 9789389716344
- Selected Stories of Rabindranath Tagore by Tagore, ISBN: 9789380914770
- Siddhartha by Hermann Hesse, ISBN: 9789380914145
- Student's Encyclopedia of G.K. by GP Editors, ISBN: 9789380914190
- Success Through a Positive Mental Attitude by N. Hill, ISBN: 9789390492435
- Tales from Shakespeare by Charles Lamb & Mary Lamb, ISBN: 9789380914367
- The Art of War by Sun Tzu, ISBN: 9789380914893
- The Autobiography of a Yogi by Paramahansa Yogananda, ISBN: 9789380914602
- The Book of Enoch by Enoch, ISBN: 9789390492480
- The Diary of a Young Girl by Anne Frank, ISBN: 9789380914312
- The Dynamic Laws of Prosperity by Catherine Ponder, ISBN: 9789388118156
- The Elements of Style by William Strunk, ISBN: 9789389157123
- The Game of Life and How to Play It by Florence Shinn, ISBN: 9789387669390
- The Law of Success by Napoleon Hill, ISBN: 9788180320927

Develop your reading habit | **Gift books to your friends**

OTHER BOOKS YOU MAY LIKE

- The Light of Asia by Sir Edwin Arnold, ISBN: 9789380914923
- The Mysterious Affair at Styles by Agatha Christie, ISBN: 9789390492510
- The Origin of Species by Charles Darwin, ISBN: 9788180320453
- The Plague by Albert Camus, ISBN: 9788194764892
- The Power of Positive Thinking by Norman Vincent Peale, ISBN: 9789388118569
- The Power of Your Subconscious Mind by Joseph Murphy, ISBN: 9788180320958
- The Problem of Increasing Human Energy by Nikola Tesla, ISBN: 9789354990953
- The Prophet by Kahlil Gibran, ISBN: 9789380914022
- The Psychopathology of Everyday Life by Sigmund Freud, ISBN: 9789388118071
- The Railway Children by E Nesbit, ISBN: 9789354990960
- The Red Badge of Courage by Stephen Crane, ISBN: 9789354990977
- The Richest Man in Babylon by George S. Clason, ISBN: 9789387669369
- The Science of Getting Rich by Wallace D. Wattles, ISBN: 9788180320972
- The Sound and the Fury by William Faulkner, ISBN: 9789390492572
- The Stranger by Albert Camus, ISBN: 9789390492589
- The Sun Also Rises by Ernest Hemingway, ISBN: 9789354990984
- The World as I See It by Albert Einstein, ISBN: 9789388118125
- The Yoga Sutras of Patanjali by Patanjali, ISBN: 9789389716351
- Their Eyes Were Watching God by Zora Neale Hurston, ISBN: 9788194764885
- Think and Grow Rich by Napoleon Hill, ISBN: 9788180320255
- Thought Vibration by William Walker Atkinson, ISBN: 9789389157154
- To the Lighthouse by Virginia Woolf, ISBN: 9789390492190
- Who were the Shudras by Dr B.R. Ambedkar, ISBN: 9789354991028
- World's Best Short Stories: Volume 1 by Various Authors, ISBN: 9789390492275
- Wuthering Heights by Emily Brontë, ISBN: 9788193545898
- Zen in the Art of Archery by Eugen Herrigel, ISBN: 9789354991059

Develop your reading habit | **Gift books to your friends**

www.ingramcontent.com/pod-product-compliance
Ingram Content Group UK Ltd.
Pitfield, Milton Keynes, MK11 3LW, UK
UKHW040229300826
14791UKWH00001B/67